Images

Gaynor Ramsey

Contents

To the teacher

Images is a collection of visuals, each of which is accompanied by stimuli, designed specifically to encourage students to explore their reactions, their memories, and their feelings past and present, and also to speculate about what might exist beyond what they can actually see in the book. The visuals cover a wide range of topic areas, which can all be treated to varying degrees of personal involvement. Each unit becomes more personal and more demanding in terms of emotional involvement with the topic as students proceed through the work. The written stimuli for each visual are divided into sections so that if either teacher or students should sense that they do not want to continue with the topic, the end of each of these sections provides a convenient point for stopping, without leaving a feeling of having left something unfinished. The topics give learners the opportunity to talk about subjects and concepts which are often neglected in course books and classrooms, and also to consider everyday topics from a more meaningful angle. The topics do not demand an intellectual approach and are applicable to learners from the age of about 16 upwards.

WHAT DOES A UNIT LOOK LIKE?

Each unit has the visual on the left-hand side of a double spread, with the written stimuli on the right-hand side. Thus, each double spread is a complete entity and is totally independent of the units that come before or after. The units are not graded and so there is no need to work chronologically through the book. The written material in each unit purposefully and gradually progresses from a fairly guided interpretation of the picture, through a phase of imaginative speculation about what can be seen, to a personal comment on the students' own experience of the situation, topic or concept presented. At the end of each unit there is an imaginative written task intended to give the students an opportunity to get some invaluable practice in free writing.

Here is a brief description of the sections which appear in the units:

Think about the picture. This first section serves to focus the learners' attention on particular aspects of the visual, by means of guiding questions with suggested reactions, as well as the complete freedom to react differently. In nearly all of these sections there is no right or wrong answer. This section is invaluable to students who may not be used to letting their imaginations be very active or to speculating widely, in that they get some suggestions as to a direction that could be taken. This section could be used by students individually as a preparation for other work to come, or could be used in groups or with the class as a whole.

Use your imagination. Questions are presented here which are designed to push the learner beyond the actual scene of the visual. Again, there are no right or wrong answers and it is hoped that everyone concerned will get away from the factual, obvious question and answer routine which often features in foreign language learning. In this section, the students' use of imagination is unlimited. If they see a poor man, their speculation as to why he is poor, if he's always been poor, if he chooses to be poor, how he copes with being poor etc. can go on and on, even though they have no concrete information about him. This section can be worked on in pairs, in small groups or with the whole class pooling ideas. Individual work should be avoided here as a train of thought or a series of connections between ideas rarely develop dynamically or quickly unless fed and stimulated by ideas from others.

Talk to a partner and **Group opinion**. These two sections both appear in nearly all of the units. As their titles suggest, classes are now divided into pairs or into small groups (ideally of 3 or 4 people) for various activities. The groupwork is in the form of some sort of task connected by theme to the topic of the unit. This task includes such activities as list-making, list-sorting, story-building, vocabulary explanations and discussions. The **Talk to a partner** section is in the form of guided interviews (which may or may not be used for reporting back) and in some cases dialogue-building and mini role play. These sections provide an opportunity for all students to be busy talking and exchanging ideas in the somewhat sheltered atmosphere of a small group.

What about you? This section extends an invitation to the students to delve into their memories and feelings, and examine how the contents of the unit relate to them personally. If the topic is such that a group of students may not want to reveal their innermost feelings, and are not willing or able to take part in such a personal exchange with each other, this section could be left out or only used selectively.

Write about it. A written task is included at the end of each unit, and should be used at the end of the work on the unit so that each student has had the chance to collect information and ideas from others and has also had time to explore, add to and perhaps modify his/her own opinions and attitudes. The tasks vary from letter-writing and descriptive writing to writing instructions and factual reports. The length of the written work is flexible: there are only a few units where the length is restricted by the task itself (e.g. writing a postcard). This written element of the material also gives an opportunity for vocabulary development (see below).

This now completes the section by section description of the units.

The vocabulary load in the written stimuli varies, with some units having specific vocabulary development tasks and others presenting topic-based vocabulary. There is a double-purpose vocabulary section at the back of the book which
a) gives suggestions to the teacher on the main vocabulary areas that could arise as part of the work on the topic
b) gives a short list of vocabulary items that may be useful to the student when doing the written tasks. The students' attention should be drawn to the existence of this section.

Neither of these vocabulary lists are intended to be prescriptive in any way, but are there as suggestions which will probably lead on to further ideas coming from the students or from the teacher. The vocabulary work that develops out of each unit will, of course, depend very much on the direction of thought about the topic and so will probably vary quite a lot from class to class. In order to be able to express themselves effectively and meaningfully about the topics in *Images* students should already have been introduced to: the present simple and present continuous tenses; the past simple and past continuous tenses/used to/ago; would like to; reported speech; future simple/going to; modals; comparatives/superlatives; present perfect simple and continuous; conditionals.

Before using a unit of this material, the teacher should take the time to go through the process of exploration of the topic. If the students are not used to working in such a free and imaginative way they might, particularly at the beginning, need some prompting and encouragement from the teacher – although, in general, the very nature of the material demands that the teacher fades very much into the background (which gives him/her the chance to monitor language production and possibly plan some remedial work for later) or just takes part in the activities with the students, without having a management role. In order to be able to encourage and prompt where needed, the teacher needs to have speculated, explored, remembered and asked himself/herself the questions in advance.

The intention behind these materials is that groups of people have the opportunity to use a language they are learning to communicate amongst themselves about meaningful topics and to talk about the connections between what is in the book, the world around them and themselves.

To the student

When we look at pictures of any kind, memories, feelings and questions often arise. A picture may bring back a scene that we have not recalled for a long time. A picture may make us feel happy, optimistic, pessimistic, sad, angry – it may make us laugh, smile or cry. A picture may make us ask for more – What happened before the moment shown in the picture? What happened after that moment? What else would we be able to see if the picture showed more? What else exists in the lives of those people – apart from the one instant we can see in the picture?

Images is a collection of visuals, each one with written material which will guide you to see more than is actually in the picture, to speculate about the situation and the people and to express yourself in a more personal way about the theme, situation or concept shown. Through using the material your ability to express yourself will increase, and so will your willingness to express yourself. You'll soon find that you feel much more confident about discussing your opinions and sharing them with others. You'll discover things about other people, and also possibly about yourself, that you didn't know before.

For Ron

Think about the picture

Why do you think these two people are here?

☐ they live here   ☐ they're spending a holiday here

☐ they're just passing through

Where do you think this picture was taken?

☐ in the suburb of a town   ☐ in a village in the mountains

☐ in a popular tourist place   ☐ . . . .

☐ in a village by the sea

As far as you can tell from the photo, what things please you about this place? Is there anything you don't like?

Use your imagination

Where are these two people staying? What sort of holiday are they spending here? What have they got in the bag that the man is carrying? What are they looking at, to the left? If these people come from a large town, how are their days different here? What do they do in the evenings in this place? Do they miss anything? Do they behave differently here? What sort of people live in this village? Describe the village and the surrounding areas.

Group opinion

Work in groups of 3 or 4.
When we are in a new place, meet a new person, or see something we have never seen before, we often want to discover certain things quite quickly – things which are important for us to know. What do you think the two people in the picture wanted to find out when they arrived at this village?

What would you like to find out as soon as possible about the following things or people?

- a house you might buy
- a large city you're visiting for the first time
- a seaside holiday resort you're staying in for the first time
- a person you might want to share your flat with
- a person you might give a job to
- a hotel you're going to stay in
- a job you might take
- a person you're falling in love with

What about you?

Tell the others about a place you've been to which was very different from the place where you live.

What sort of exploring or discovering do you most enjoy doing? What do you like experimenting with?

Write about it

You are on holiday in the place you can see in the photo. Write a postcard to a friend telling him/her about the village. You've got room for 50–60 words.

Think about the picture   Describe what you can see in this picture.

How does this picture make you feel?

☐ sorry for the people

☐ guilty because you have more food, money and possessions

☐ that you'd like to live more simply

☐ that they must be more satisfied than you

☐ that they must be less satisfied than you

☐ that the family must be very close

☐ . . . .

What do you think the relationship between these people is? What is each person's role in the family?

Use your imagination   Describe the home these people live in. What is their village or town like? How do they spend the day? What does the little girl play with? What sort of future will the baby have if it is a) a boy b) a girl? What do these people eat? What do they do in the evenings?

Group opinion   Work in groups of 3 or 4.
Find as many differences as you can between the lives of the people in the picture and your lives. Consider:

work	clothes	money
entertainment	possessions	education
travel	religion	family life

Do you think they are poorer than you in all ways?

Talk to a partner   Talk to a partner and find out

- if he/she ever does anything to help people who are poorer in some way
- when his/her way of life was most simple
- what he/she understands by simple food, simple clothes, simple wishes (with examples)
- what he/she would miss if we were all forced to live like the people in the picture

What about you?   How do you react when you come face to face with people who are obviously much less fortunate than you in some way?

Write about it   Your friend has decided to go and live in a very simple society. Write a letter telling him/her about your reactions to these plans.

Think about the picture

Which of the following do you think is correct?

☐ the girl is sitting alone   ☐ she is at home

☐ she is with other people   ☐ she is in a public place

What has she received by post?

☐ a bill   ☐ an advertising leaflet

☐ an invitation   ☐ a personal letter

Which of these words do you think could describe her reaction?

☐ puzzled   ☐ relieved   ☐ disappointed

☐ happy   ☐ angry   ☐ . . . .

☐ sad   ☐ thoughtful

Who do you think the letter is from? What are its contents?

Use your imagination

When did she receive the letter? Where is she, if she isn't at home? When did she open the letter? Is it written by hand or typed? Is it long or short? Was she expecting to receive this letter? What is she going to do as a result of this letter? Has her mood changed in the last few minutes? How might this letter influence the rest of her day? Will she read it once and then put it away? Will she forget about it quickly? What can she do if she is alone somewhere and this letter has really troubled her?

Talk to a partner

Talk to a partner and find out

- when he/she last received a personal letter, who it was from and what the contents were (in general!)
- if the postman is very important to him/her
- how and when the post is delivered to his/her home
- when he/she last received a bill and what it was for
- how he/she feels about sending holiday postcards
- what sort of system or habits he/she has for dealing with post
- what sort of envelopes he/she doesn't like opening

What about you?

Do you like receiving letters? Do you like writing them? What does your post mainly consist of? Do you prefer to telephone friends or write to them? Why? Who do you find it difficult to write to? What sort of letters are difficult to write?

Write about it

Write a short letter that you think could be in the girl's hands in the photo.

UNIT 4

Think about the picture   What is your reaction when you see this picture?

- [ ] it looks very cold   [ ] horrible
- [ ] I'd like to stay indoors and look out at the snow   [ ] lovely
- [ ] I'd like to go and play in the snow   [ ] . . . .
- [ ] it's never like that where I live

What can you see when you look out of your window in winter?

Use your imagination   Where are all the people who live in these houses? What are they doing? Why do people come to this place? How do they spend their days here? What special things could people do here at this time of the year? What do people bring with them when they come here? What would this picture be like if it were in colour? What would this scene be like in summer?

Talk to a partner   Talk to a partner and find out

- which season of the year he/she prefers and why
- what experience he/she has had of a) snow b) winter holidays c) winter sports
- how he/she likes to spend cold winter weekends
- what the climate of his/her country is like
- what sort of climate he/she would most like to live in

Group opinion   Work in groups of 3 or 4.
Make a detailed contrast of the two most extreme seasons of summer and winter. Here are some ideas about the aspects you could consider:

- the food we eat   • light and temperature
- the clothes we wear   • our work
- the way we spend our free time

Talk to another partner   With a partner, make a list of as many words as you can think of that can be used to talk about the weather. Compare your list with those of the others.

What about you?   Is the weather and the time of the year very important to you? When do you feel most comfortable and at your best? Does the weather have any influence on your health and the way you feel in general? Do you believe that weather conditions can influence people's well-being and their behaviour?

Write about it   A friend from abroad is coming to visit you. Write a letter telling him/her about the weather at the moment and the clothes that would be suitable.

UNIT 5

Think about the picture   What type of phone can you see in this picture?

☐ a very modern one   ☐ a rather old-fashioned one

☐ a type you've seen before   ☐ one that is pleasant to use

The following things can be seen on some phones. Are they on this one?

☐ a dial   ☐ a slot   ☐ instructions for use

☐ a receiver   ☐ buttons   ☐ the number of the phone

What are the differences between this phone and the one that you most often use? Which do you think is better?

Use your imagination   Where is this phone? Who uses it? What sort of conversations is it used for (private, business, long, short, local, long-distance etc.)? What can be seen under the phone? What are these things used for? When a person uses this phone, what might he or she do physically? This phone is ringing now, and you can hear it – where are you, what are you doing and what is your reaction to the ringing of the phone?

Talk to a partner   Talk to a partner and find out

* how he/she feels about using the phone
* what experience he/she has had of telephone answering machines
* how often he/she uses the phone, and for what purpose
* if he/she ever refuses to answer the phone and just lets it ring and ring

Number the following in the order in which they might happen when making a phone call from a private phone to a large company.

. . . the line suddenly goes dead

. . . a secretary tells you it's the wrong office

. . . you look up the number in the phone book

. . . a secretary asks you to hang on

. . . you are put through to a department

. . . the telephonist apologizes for the mistake and says she'll put you through to another office

. . . you mutter a complaint to yourself, and decide to try another company

. . . you are transferred back to the switchboard

. . . you ask for a particular extension

. . . you hear the ringing tone

. . . you redial the number

. . . the telephonist speaks to you

. . . you hang up angrily

. . . you dial the number

. . . you replace the receiver

. . . you hear the engaged tone

. . . the phone is answered

Now make groups of 3, and reconstruct the dialogue!

What about you?   Tell the others about a couple of phone calls that you can remember very clearly because they were special or unusual in some way. Try to explain how you felt about these calls.

Write about it   Write clear instructions telling someone how to use the public phones that exist in your country.

Think about the picture Is your reaction to the situation shown in this picture positive or negative? What are the reasons for this reaction?

positive reaction:	negative reaction:
☐ not crowded	☐ modern building
☐ modern building	☐ style of paintings
☐ combination of paintings and sculptures	☐ dislike of museums and art galleries in general
☐	☐ . . . .

What have all the pictures and sculptures here got in common with each other? What sort of paintings do you like?

Use your imagination Why are there so few people here? How long has the woman been sitting on the stool? What is she doing? What other things might the girl on the left do before leaving the gallery? Describe the interior of this building. Are there stairs, lifts, escalators, windows, permanent walls? Which other people are probably in the building at this moment? Describe what the front of the sculpture of the woman and child could be like.

Talk to a partner Talk to a partner and find out

- what sort of things he/she has got on the walls at home
- which form of art he/she most likes: paintings, sculptures, drawings, photos etc.
- if he/she has any trouble understanding 'modern art'
- if he/she is a creative person in any way

What about you? When did you last go into a museum or art gallery? What was your reason for going there?

☐ the weather was bad	☐ someone else wanted to go
☐ you wanted to see something in particular	☐ it was free
☐ you were just generally interested	☐ . . . .

Describe a museum or art gallery you have been to. Tell the others about the things you saw and your general impression of the place. How many galleries and museums of any kind and in any country can your class collect together and describe?

Write about it You work in a very large old palace, part of which is now an art gallery and museum too. In the last few years you've noticed that schoolchildren in groups have become badly behaved. Write a list of rules and regulations that you can send to the teachers before they bring their classes to the palace. Include any information that you think will help to improve the situation.

Think about the picture

This man is busy doing something. Do you think

a) it's ☐ part of his job ☐ a hobby ☐ related to his work in some way?

b) he does this ☐ every day ☐ once or twice a week

☐ in the evening ☐ in the daytime?

c) he can ☐ only listen here ☐ listen and speak?

d) he is ☐ concentrating hard ☐ enjoying himself ☐ thinking about something else?

What exactly is this man doing here? How does this activity fit in with the rest of his learning process?

Use your imagination

How many other people are in the room? Is the room comfortable? How is it decorated? What is this man sitting on? Where is the teacher sitting? What is he or she doing? What can be heard in the room? What would you be able to see if you stood at the back of the room? What kind of atmosphere is there in the room?

Group opinion

Work in groups of 3 or 4.
Compare the following ways of learning a language:

- learning by yourself – with a dictionary
  - with a cassette course
  - with a correspondence course
- using – a language laboratory
  - a computer
- learning by – doing translations
  - doing grammar exercises
  - speaking all the time
- learning – with a teacher
  - without a teacher
- going to school to learn English – in your own country
  - in a country where English is spoken

Are there any methods here that everybody in the group thinks are good or bad? Tell the group about the experiences you've had learning English (or another foreign language).

Talk to a partner

Talk to a partner and ask him or her to use the following words and expressions about his or her schooldays:

favourite subject	hate	homework	punishment	favourite teacher
schoolfriend	sports	best memory	most boring	classroom

What about you?

Ask the question 'What about you?' to your teacher. Try to find out what his/her attitude towards teaching English is. Get him/her to talk about the experience he/she has had, and the feeling he/she has about the materials available and the school where you are learning now.

Write about it

Someone in your English class is in hospital. Write a short letter to him or her, describing what you did in the last lesson.

UNIT *8*

Think about the picture   What do you think these two policemen are doing?

☐ going to start their day's work   ☐ going home

☐ walking to the scene of a crime they've   ☐ watching the people in the
     been called to   streets

What impression of them do you get?

☐ they're in a hurry   ☐ they're following someone

☐ they're on their way to a particular place   ☐ they're just walking around

What do you think might be the good and the bad aspects of being one of these policemen?

Use your imagination   What was the first thing these policemen did when they started work today? What orders were they given? Which part of the town are they walking in? Describe the street. Who lives here? How do the people react here when they see the policemen? What various problems do they have to deal with in their daily work? Where do they have lunch? Why are the two together all day? How could they defend themselves if someone attacked them? What are they talking about?

Talk to a partner   One of you is a policeman or policewoman. Act out an interview between the policeman/policewoman and one of the following people:
a) an old lady whose purse has been stolen in a supermarket
b) a man who had an accident yesterday, after drinking too much, and killed a child in the street
c) a rich woman whose diamonds have been stolen from her home

In each case ask a question beginning:
How much . . .?   Was / Were . . .?   Why . . .?   Did . . .?

Do you feel any sympathy for any of these three people? If so, why? How far were they each to blame for what happened?

Talk to another partner   Talk to another partner and find out

• if he/she has ever paid a fine (if so, what for)
• when the last time was that he/she spoke to a police officer, and the reason
• what he/she would think if a police officer in uniform knocked on the door one evening
• if he/she thinks it is a good or bad thing to have armed police officers on the street
• if he/she would consider joining the police force

What about you?   Tell the others of a good and a bad experience you've had with the police. What is the general attitude towards the police in your country?

Write about it   You witnessed one of the following crimes:
a) a man on a motorbike snatching a woman's handbag
b) a car accident
Write a report for the police.

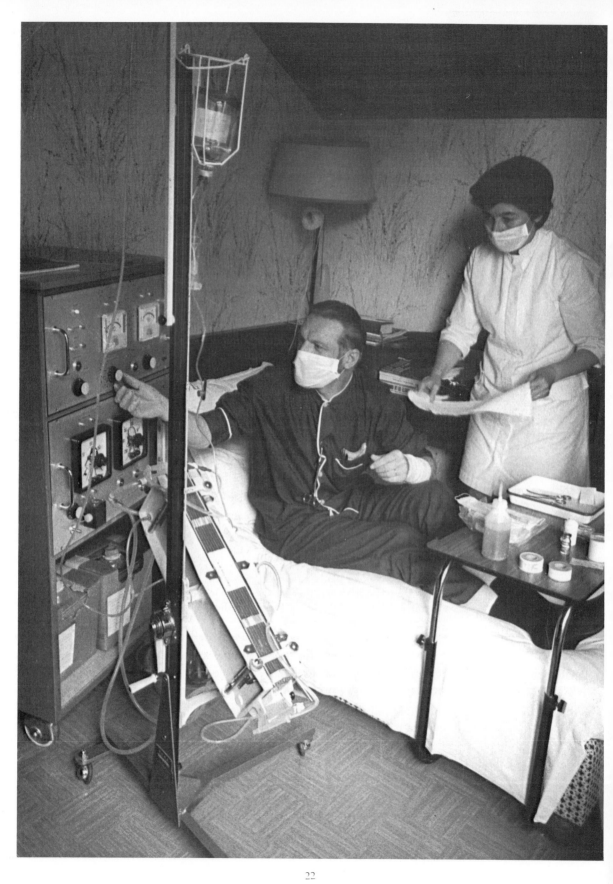

UNIT 9

Think about the picture

This man is ☐ at home ☐ in hospital

The woman helping him is ☐ a permanent nurse ☐ his wife

☐ a visiting nurse ☐ . . . .

This man has got something wrong with

☐ his mouth ☐ his arm ☐ an internal organ

His treatment has to be carried out

☐ when he has time ☐ regularly ☐ only if he feels ill

His illness ☐ is extremely dangerous for him

☐ can be kept under control by these machines

☐ could kill him at some time in the future

☐ influences his day-to-day life a lot

☐ is relatively unimportant to him

What's the matter with this man? What does he need these machines for?

Use your imagination

Is this treatment very complicated or painful to carry out? Describe all the things you can see in this room. What else might there be in the room? What or who would definitely not be allowed into the room? What can the woman do to help him? If he has got young children, how do they feel about this room? If his children are teenagers, how do they feel? Why does he prefer to use these machines at home rather than in a hospital? Where did he get the machines from? Were they cheap? How could he afford to pay for them? What might happen if the machines went wrong? Why are they wearing masks?

Talk to a partner

Talk to a partner and find out

- if he/she is in good health
- if he/she pays much attention to fitness and health
- if he/she is good at looking after other people when they are ill
- some details about the last time he/she was ill or went to see a doctor

Group opinion

Work in groups of 3 or 4.
There are many things in our world today that can help to ruin our health – if we allow them to. Make a list of as many of these things as you can. How could an individual avoid some of these risks? Are any of them impossible to avoid?

What about you?

What experience have you had of hospitals, as a visitor, a patient or an employee? Tell the others about an illness, operation or accident you've had.

Write about it

Write a general list of advice which you think might help to keep people healthy, e.g. Eat a piece of fruit every day.
Don't go to bed without cleaning your teeth.

Think about the picture
What sort of people do you think these hands belong to?

☐ a baby ☐ a man ☐ a boy ☐ a girl ☐ a woman

Are they young, middle-aged or old? What do you think could be the relationship between the two people?

Use your imagination
Describe the appearance of the two people. What sort of clothes are they wearing? Where are these people? What's the room like? Are there any other people in the room? What other things do these two do together? How are these two important for each other? Will their relationship stay the same over the years or will it change? How could it perhaps change?

Talk to a partner
Talk to a partner and find out

- if he/she has ever liked doing jigsaw puzzles
- what his/her favourite toy was as a child
- if he/she has still got a toy from his/her childhood
- what sort of toys he/she would still like to play with
- which toys he/she thinks are particularly good or particularly bad for children

Talk to another partner
Finish these questions that the child might ask the other person in this picture:

How many . . . . ?

Where . . . . ?

Can I . . . . ?

What do you think the answers could be?

What about you?
What good experience can you remember having with an older person (e.g. grandmother, neighbour etc.) when you were a child? Describe how you felt about this person. Can you remember not liking or being afraid of a person because they were old? Describe all the grandparents that you knew (or still know now).

Write about it
Use some of the following words to describe the situation you can see in the picture:

rainy day	jigsaw puzzle	too young
complicated	chair	patient
birthday present	pieces	educational
help	holiday	co-ordination

You can, of course, use other vocabulary too if there is something else you want to express.

Think about the picture
How expensive do you think the food in this restaurant is?

☐ cheap ☐ medium-priced ☐ rather expensive

What sort of people are here?

☐ young people ☐ families ☐ older people

What is the general atmosphere of this restaurant?

☐ elegant ☐ snobbish ☐ international

☐ simple ☐ friendly ☐ local

What time of year do you think it is? What day, and what time of day is it? Would you like to eat in this restaurant? If so, why? If not, why not?

Use your imagination
What sort of food does this restaurant serve? What is the speciality of the house? Why do people enjoy coming here? Where is this restaurant situated? What is the restaurant building like? Who runs this restaurant? What might these people do after they've enjoyed their meal? What are the disadvantages of a restaurant like this? Are there any special advantages? What are the customers enjoying, apart from the food?

Talk to a partner
Talk to a partner and find out

- when he/she last ate in a restaurant and whether the meal was enjoyable
- what type of restaurant he/she most likes and most dislikes
- what he/she would choose for a special birthday dinner
- which sort of foreign food he/she enjoys very much
- how many details he/she can remember about the picture (without looking back at it!)

Talk to another partner
Arrange the following words (that all have something to do with food or with restaurants) into categories and give each category a title. Then try to add at least one more word, if possible two more words, to each category.

main course	menu	serviette	spoon
manager	waiter	chef	wine list
frying pan	salad servers	cork	kettle
salt and pepper	wine glass	fork	waitress
knife	saucepan	tablecloth	dessert

What about you?
A lot of people in the world haven't got enough to eat. How do you feel about the amount of food you and your friends or family eat?

Make some comments about your eating habits. Would you like to make any changes?

Write about it
Write down a recipe for a simple dish – the recipe should include a list of ingredients and instructions.

28

UNIT 12

Think about the picture

Where do you think these flats are?

☐ in the country ☐ in the middle of a town ☐ in a suburb

Who do you think these flats are most suitable for?

☐ older people ☐ families with children

☐ young people ☐ couples with no children

Would you like to live here? If so, why? If not, why not? What do you think could be good about living in a place like this? What may be bad?

Use your imagination

What do the people who live in these flats use their balconies for? What is the view from the windows of these flats like? Describe the flats – are the rooms big or small? What are the walls like? And the floors? Are the kitchens modern? What about the bathrooms? Describe in detail everything you see when you come to visit a friend here – start with the place where you park your car, then the things you walk past on your way to the building, then the entrance to the building etc. Where are these flats? Is the building well built? What about the interior of the building – light, heating, noise etc.?

Talk to a partner

Talk to a partner and find out

- how he/she feels about the room you're both in now
- what he/she would like to change at home
- what the ideal home would be for him/her
- how important the home is for him/her

Group opinion

Think of situations in which a person might feel happy, depressed, grateful, lonely or relieved about finding a flat in this building. Make up a short story describing the background to each of these situations.

What about you?

What are the most important points for you when you're looking for somewhere to live? Tell the others of experiences you've had while home-hunting or when looking for a place to stay just for a short time.

Write about it

A friend of yours is arriving today – you've already arranged, by letter, that he/she can stay in your home and that you will be there at the time agreed by both of you. Unfortunately you have been suddenly called away on business – and, as you live alone, your home is empty. You'll be back in three days. You have left the key with a neighbour. Write a message to your friend giving all the information you think might be necessary or helpful about your home and the neighbourhood.

Think about the picture

Who do you think these two young people are?

☐ relatives   ☐ friends   ☐ lovers

☐ they work together   ☐ strangers

What are they talking about?

☐ something personal and private   ☐ a business matter

☐ a matter of public interest   ☐ something important to them

☐ a topic of no real importance to them

What role do you think each is playing in the conversation? Is one of them more defensive than the other? Is one more intense about the conversation than the other? What impression do you get of their feelings at the moment this photo was taken?

Use your imagination

Where is this conversation taking place? Why are these people here?
What is the weather like? What time of year is it? What are other people nearby doing? What were these two doing an hour ago? What might they do when they've finished their conversation?

Talk to a partner

What do you think the two young people are talking about? Use some of the ideas below to describe the phases of the conversation.

What happened before this conversation?	What is happening during this conversation?	What will happen before the end of this conversation?
something positive something negative something unexpected nothing special	someone is making a suggestion they are having an argument one of them is saying 'yes' one of them is saying 'no' one is persuading the other	they'll agree on something they'll disagree they'll make a promise they'll make some arrangements for the future

How will they feel after the conversation – happy, sad, satisfied, dissatisfied?

What about you?

Who would you talk to if you were worried about   a) your work   b) your health   c) money   d) a relationship with another person? How many people do you know who you can really talk to about intimate and personal problems?

Write about it

You have got a personal problem (it can be to do with work, home, a relationship with another person or a difficult decision of any sort). Write a short letter to the 'problem page' in a magazine. Describe the situation and ask for some advice.

UNIT *14*

Think about the picture   What's your reaction when you see this picture of an airport?

☐ you think back to your last holiday

☐ you wish you could go away now

☐ you suddenly think of planning your next holiday

☐ you feel glad you're not flying today

☐ you think positively about airport atmosphere

☐ you think negatively about airport atmosphere

☐ you think about terrorists

☐ . . . .

Close your eyes. Describe something you can imagine hearing at the airport. Explain what this sound is, and how it is being made or who is making it.

Use your imagination   Which people are inside the plane you can see at the moment? What are they doing? Where is the pilot? Where are the flight attendants and the passengers? What are they all doing? What has to be done to or in the plane before it takes off? How do the passengers feel at the moment? What are they perhaps worrying about? Where are they going? What things have they packed to take with them?

Talk to a partner   Talk to a partner and find out

- if he/she has flown before (if so, how many times and where to)
- what he/she likes most about flying
- what he/she dislikes most about flying
- how he/she compares flying with other ways of travelling

Group opinion   Work in groups of 3 or 4.
These words all have something to do with making a journey by plane. Number them in the order in which you would have to use them to describe a flight. Give a short explanation for each of the words.

. . . to take off	. . . passport control	. . . seat belt
. . . runway	. . . check-in desk	. . . boarding card
. . . security check	. . . airport bus	. . . passenger lounge
. . . aisle	. . . duty-free shop	. . . customs
. . . to land	. . . flight attendant	. . . emergency instructions
. . . packed meal or snack	. . . luggage reclaim	. . . gate

What about you?   Tell the others of a good and/or bad experience you've had at an airport or in a plane.

At which stages of a journey by plane can you imagine having the following feelings?
sadness   nervousness   boredom   relief   impatience   fear   happiness

Write about it   You have picked up a suggestion card at a large international airport. Write a suggestion for something that would improve the airport. You can write 50–60 words.

UNIT 15

Think about the picture

This scene is from a film. When do you think it was made?

☐ before 1950   ☐ in the sixties   ☐ in the eighties

☐ in the fifties   ☐ in the seventies

What are the two people looking at? A scene they find

☐ sad   ☐ amusing   ☐ shocking

☐ worrying   ☐ exciting   ☐ . . . .

What is the general atmosphere in the picture like?

☐ one of optimism   ☐ one of pessimism   ☐ . . . .

If you know which famous film this scene comes from, tell as much as you can of the story. If you don't know, look at page 64.

Use your imagination

What could these two people be looking at if the window overlooked a lake, a busy road, a side street, the sea? Describe, in detail, the room and the building these people are in. What were they doing before they came to the window to look out? What are they each thinking now?

Talk to a partner

Talk to a partner and find out

- when he/she last saw a film in a cinema and on television
- who his/her favourite actor and actress are or used to be
- which type of film he/she doesn't like watching
- which his/her favourite film is and what it's about

Group opinion

Work in groups of 3 or 4.
What are some of the typical characteristics of the following types of film?

a western	a James Bond film	a horror film
a love story	a comedy	a documentary film
a war film	a criminal film	

What about you?

How do you feel about watching films in a cinema? Is it better in any way than watching them on television at home? Would you like to have a video?

What forms of entertainment do you like the most? Why?

Write about it

Write a short paragraph describing what you saw and what was going on when you walked into a cinema, theatre, opera house, classical concert hall, pop concert hall or jazz club.

Think about the picture   Which contrasts seen here are the most interesting for you?

☐ the speed of the car and the cart

☐ the surface of the path and the road

☐ the way of life of the man with the cart and the driver of the car

☐ . . . .

Where do you think this photo was taken?

Use your imagination   What has the man got on his cart? Where's he going? Where's he come from? What does he look like? What's his job? Why doesn't he transport his things by car? How does he feel about the 'modern invention' – the car? What other aspects of his life might not have changed as they have for most people? In what ways is his life probably different from that of the driver of the car?

Group opinion   Work in groups of 3 or 4.
Which things have changed a lot in our lifetime? What changes would an 80-year-old person be able to tell us about? Choose one of the following and tell the story of the slow developments:

● from typist to company director
● from waitress to society lady
● from poor man to rich man
● from rich man to poor man

Which of these changes could also be very fast?

Talk to a partner   Talk to a partner and ask him/her

● to describe something that is continuously developing or changing in his/her life
● to describe a moment in his/her life when a decision was made that brought about a change (sudden or slow)
● if there is anything he/she would like to change about himself/herself

What about you?   Tell the others about something that exists either in your personal life or in society that you would like to see changed. Do you think it will be possible to change this? If so, how?

Write about it   Choose one of the following modern inventions which you think has some advantages but also some disadvantages. Write a paragraph about the positive and the negative aspects of one of these:
television   telephone   computer   video   car   plane

Think about the picture

Do you think this man is

☐ on his way to work?

☐ on his way home from work?

☐ going on holiday?

☐ on a day trip?

☐ going to Sidcup for the first time?

☐ travelling alone?

☐ with someone?

Do you think he has chosen a good method of making sure he gets off the train at the right place?

Use your imagination

What's this man's job? What's his daily routine? Why is he so tired? What is there outside the train he's sitting in? Describe the man's clothes. What can be heard outside the train? What can be heard inside the train? What are the other passengers doing to pass the time? What risk is the man taking?

Group opinion

Do you think the following are to be found at a station or on a train?

left luggage
luggage rack
ticket office

barrier
ticket collector
communication cord

compartment
corridor

Describe each one, including its appearance and function.

Talk to a partner

Talk to a partner and find out

- how often he/she travels by train when living at home
- if he/she has ever travelled by train in another country
- if he/she likes travelling by train
- details about the longest train journey he/she has ever made
- if he/she has ever been a train commuter like the man in the picture

Group opinion

The man in the train has written a message for another person to read. What information might be left in messages left by the following people:

- wife to husband (she had to leave the house suddenly before he got home from work)
- teacher to students (the teacher suddenly had to drive another student to a hospital)
- visitor to friend (the visitor, who has stayed overnight, gets up late and leaves after the friend has gone to work)

What about you?

What special methods have you got to make sure you don't forget things? Do you ever make lists? How do you remember to pay bills, to send birthday cards and to reply to letters? How do you remember to take all the things you need with you when you leave the house? Is there anything you often forget?

Write about it

Write the story of something you once forgot, and the consequences of forgetting it.

UNIT *18*

Think about the picture What do you think must be the worst thing about working here?

☐ the heat   ☐ the type of work   ☐ the surroundings

☐ the noise   ☐ the lack of contact   ☐ . . . .
                           between the women

Who could the woman in the background be?

☐ an employee who has left her sewing machine for a while

☐ a visitor   ☐ a supervisor

☐ the boss   ☐ . . . .

Use your imagination What are these women doing? What is their daily routine? How often do they have a break? How is their salary calculated? How do these women feel about the job they're doing? Why aren't there any men here? Which other people could be working elsewhere in this building? What can be heard, smelt and seen in this room? What other rooms might these women go into during the day? What would be the function of a supervisor working here?

Talk to a partner Interview a partner about his/her job (past, present or imagined). Find out about

- the work he/she does
- the surroundings and facilities such as a canteen or sports club
- the advantages of the job
- the disadvantages of the job
- his/her colleagues at work

Group opinion Work in groups of 3 or 4.
Make lists of the five most important points you would include in a description of:

a good employer   a good employee
a bad employer   a bad employee

Talk to another partner Tell each other about jobs you've had – as a part of training, temporary jobs, student holiday jobs etc. Discuss the ideas you have about 'dream jobs'.

What about you? Which jobs do you think would be so boring, so dangerous, so demanding or so unpleasant that you wouldn't want to do them?

How would you (or did you) feel before, during and after an interview for a job? What questions and thoughts might go through your mind in each of these three phases?

What are your aims (if any) in the field of jobs and work?

Write about it You've seen an advertisement for a summer job in a first class hotel by the sea. You'd like to have this job – you want to have a complete change from what you do for the rest of the year. Write a letter to the hotel manager, telling him any details about yourself that you think would be relevant and that would make him think that you are suitable for the job.

Think about the picture

This little boy seems to have tears in his eyes. Why do you think they are there?

☐ he is sad   ☐ he is frightened of something

☐ he has been laughing   ☐ he is very happy about something

☐ he has just hurt himself   ☐ . . . .

☐ he is saying goodbye

Any of the above explanations could be true. Describe the situation that has caused the tears in each case.

Use your imagination

Where was this photo taken? What is the relationship between the two? Why is it important to them? Why has this little boy got a special place in the man's heart? What do you think the little boy is like? What about the man, what sort of person is he? What things do they do together? Is this little boy loved? What hopes has the man got for the boy? What experiences would he like to protect him from? What is the man doing in the photo? What sort of stories does the man tell the little boy? When does he tell him these stories?

Talk to a partner

Finish these questions that the little boy might ask the man about things he doesn't understand.

Why do. . . . .?

Why does . . . .?

What was . . . .?

What did you . . . .?

Why did . . . .?

Can you tell me . . . .?

Why don't . . . .?

Will I . . . .?

. . . .?

How do you think the man would answer these questions?

Group opinion

Work in groups of 3 or 4.
Perhaps these two people are saying goodbye. Think of some situations when saying goodbye must be specially difficult or painful for one or both of the people. Have you ever said a painful goodbye?

What about you?

What are your reactions to this photograph?

Describe a close friendship you've had with another person at some time in your life. What is needed to make a relationship into a very special one?

Write about it

Write a short description of someone who was once very important or close to you but doesn't play a major part in your life anymore.

Think about the picture   When do you think this picture was taken?

☐ immediately after the people left   ☐ the next morning   ☐ a few days later

What does this picture make you think about the people who were drinking here?

☐ that they were dirty and should have cleared everything away

☐ that they'll probably come and clear up later

☐ that they left this place very late

☐ that they were all completely drunk when they left

☐ . . . .

Does it disturb you to see these things left here? Does a mess of any sort disturb you in any situation at all?

Use your imagination   Where are these tables and chairs? Who drank the contents of the bottles? What was in the bottles? What did the people do while they were drinking? Did they drink too much? What was the reason for the people meeting here? Is this someone's home or is it a bar? What did the people do after they'd finished drinking? What is the building behind the tables like? What sort of people usually come here?

Group opinion   Work in groups of 3 or 4.
It is often possible to find things still in place after the people have left (like the bottles and glasses in the photo). From these things we can often imagine what the people did there before they left. Tell in detail what the people did:

• in a small room with a lot of glass tubes and a strange smell in it
• in a room with a mattress on the floor, some rope and some old newspapers
• in the forest where you found some ashes on the ground

Think of one more situation like these that you can give to another group to comment on.

Talk to a partner   One person should close their eyes. The second should choose a drink from this list and ask the other person to describe the scene he/she imagines in his/her mind – the place, the people, the situation, what they're drinking out of and any other details.

| beer | cocktails | red wine | espresso coffee |
| tea | champagne | coca cola | mineral water |

What about you?   How do you feel about the drinking of alcohol? Have you ever drunk too much? Have you ever seen the results of other people having drunk too much? Are there situations where it is acceptable to drink, and some where it is unacceptable? What are they?

Write about it   Write a short paragraph comparing typical food and drink in your country with that of another country you have either visited or heard about.

UNIT 21

Think about the picture

What do you think the relationship is between the man who is crying and the man with his hand on his shoulder?

☐ brothers   ☐ employer and employee   ☐ friends

☐ strangers   ☐ patient and doctor   ☐ . . . .

Think of a possible explanation for why this man is crying.

Use your imagination

Where are these people? Why can you only see men in this picture? What are they doing? Describe the things and the other people that might be in this room. Is the general atmosphere one of happiness or sadness? What can happen to people if they become very sad or depressed? Who can try to help them? How? Is it good for this man to cry? Why?

Group opinion

Work in groups of 3 or 4.
People cry for various reasons and in various situations. Think of a situation in which someone might cry because they feel:

relieved   shocked   disappointed   sad
happy   afraid   frustrated

Children and babies often cry for other reasons. Can you think of any?

Talk to a partner

Talk to a partner and find out

- when the last time was that he/she cried
- how he/she feels when other people cry
- what sort of reaction is most welcome from other people if he/she cries
- in which situation he/she hates crying or thinks it's good to cry

What about you?

The men in this picture are very probably in a psychiatric clinic of some sort. If you have never seen inside such a clinic, what do you imagine it's like? Where have you got your ideas from? If you have seen inside a clinic, tell the others something about the impressions you got, the appearance of the place and the atmosphere.

Do you think that the media (particularly TV and cinema) give people an accurate picture?

Write about it

You have a friend who is obviously overworked. Write a short letter to him/her describing what you do to make yourself feel better if you are very tired or under a lot of pressure.

UNIT *22*

Think about the picture

Do you think this man's activity in the photo is

☐ his job   ☐ his hobby?

How do you think he feels at the moment?

☐ afraid   ☐ relaxed   ☐ tense   ☐ concentrated   ☐ . . . . . .

Every year many people, professionals and amateurs, die as a result of high-risk sports. Why do people choose to do such things?

Use your imagination

Who took this photo? Why was it taken? Which other people are probably nearby? What is above this man? What is below him? What special equipment or clothing has he got? Supposing he has a family, how does his wife feel about his hobby? When does he think about the risks he's taking? How is he sometimes reminded of those risks? How does he feel when he goes home after a climbing expedition? Describe the scenery of the area where this picture was taken.

Talk to a partner

Talk to a partner and find out

- what his/her main hobby is
- how far the hobby is a contrast to work or everyday life
- if he/she ever does anything that is a risk in any way
- if he/she knows anyone who takes risks in any way
- which sport he/she thinks is probably the riskiest

Group opinion

Work in groups of 3 or 4.
Taking risks need not be restricted only to sports. Consider the following list. Which of these activities do you consider to be risks? Is there anyone in the group who would not do any of them because of the risk involved?

- buying shares
- travelling in foreign countries
- travelling by plane
- smoking
- driving on a motorway

- living near a nuclear power station
- being driven home from a party late at night
- giving false information to the tax office
- riding a bicycle in a large town
- walking alone in a city at night

What about you?

What is the riskiest thing you have ever done? What was the outcome of it? Is there anything that you'd like to do, but probably wouldn't do because of the risk?

How do you feel about people who take risks and put you at risk at the same time? Do you ever consider any other people when making decisions about risks, or do you only consider yourself?

Write about it

This letter was in a newspaper last week. Write to the editor giving your reactions to it.

Dear Editor,
I'd like to comment on your recent three articles on motor racing, skiing and hang-gliding. I must say I find your articles irresponsible, to say the least! You make these sports seem glamorous and exciting – without mentioning how dangerous they are and how many people are killed because of them. They should be banned! Do you want all our young people to go out and risk their necks every weekend?
                                                    E.M., South London.

UNIT 23

Think about the picture

What sort of shop do you think Moss Bros is?

- [ ] a department store
- [ ] a wedding clothes shop
- [ ] a boutique
- [ ] a discount clothes shop
- [ ] a shop for elegant clothes
- [ ] . . . .

What are the two punks doing?

- [ ] deciding which clothes they want to buy
- [ ] admiring the clothes
- [ ] discussing getting married
- [ ] joking about something
- [ ] having a rest
- [ ] . . . .

What contrasts does this picture suggest to you?

Use your imagination

What sort of street is this? Where is it? If the picture were much bigger, what else would you see in the street? If the photo were in colour, what colours would there be in it? Describe the punks' appearance in detail. What do they do all day? Why do they dress like this? Where do they live? Are their parents punks too? How do people react when they meet people who look like this? Where might these two people not be accepted because of their appearance? Is their way of dressing just a question of fashion?

Talk to a partner

Exchange opinions on today's fashion in clothing, hair etc. Explain how you feel about fashion and clothes.

Group opinion

Work in groups of 3 or 4.
Many things have an influence on fashion for young people and on their reaction to fashion. Sort this list into the order of importance you think is realistic – beginning with the most important.

. . . advertising on posters in the street   . . . magazines and newspapers

. . . shop displays   . . . the climate

. . . royalty and other public figures   . . . pop singers

. . . the money people have   . . . high class fashion designers

. . . television serials   . . . advertising on television

Is there anything else you'd like to add to this list?

What about you?

What are the important criteria for you when you buy clothes? Is there any article of clothing you don't like shopping for? Do you ever make mistakes when shopping for clothes? Compared with now, have you ever had a very different attitude towards clothes and fashion?

Write about it

Describe the clothes you feel most comfortable in and the clothes that you feel most uncomfortable in.

UNIT 24

Think about the picture

What time of year is it in the photo?

☐ summer ☐ autumn ☐ winter ☐ spring

Why do you think this little boy is here?

☐ he lives here

☐ he's visiting someone here

☐ he doesn't know the place but just wants to play here

☐ he's running away from someone

☐ . . . .

Which of the following do you think the picture symbolizes?

☐ freedom ☐ adventure ☐ pleasure

☐ escape ☐ danger ☐ forbidden things

How do you think the little boy feels when he sees that the gate is open? What would he like to do?

Use your imagination

Describe the inside of the house in as much detail as you can. Are there any other buildings on this piece of land? What's the garden like? What's the area around the house like? What sort of road goes past the house? Are there any other people in the house at the moment? If so, what are they doing? What is the little boy like as a person? What's his family like? Why is he playing alone? What dangers could he possibly meet if he left the garden? Who left the gate open?

Talk to a partner

Doors open and close in many different ways. Work out a description of how the following doors work and comment on where they are often found.

sliding doors	revolving doors	swing doors
ordinary doors	automatic doors	remote control doors

Group opinion

Work in groups of 3 or 4.
Decide whether you prefer to see the following doors open or closed:

- the door to the dentist's surgery
- the classroom door a minute before the lesson begins
- your house door when you come home
- your bedroom door
- the gate to a park
- the safe door at the bank
- a cathedral door
- your bathroom door
- lift doors

What difference does it make to you if these doors are open or closed?

What about you?

What can open doors symbolize? And closed doors? Do you see one of these as positive and the other negative? Has any particular door ever meant anything special to you? Which door or doors might you feel afraid of opening and walking through?

Write about it

Continue this dramatic short story:
She walked hesitatingly up to the door. Nervously, she raised her hand to knock – but her hand remained frozen in mid-air when, through the door, she heard . . .

UNIT 25

Think about the picture   What do you think this photograph was used for?

☐ an advertisement for
. . . .

☐ to blackmail either the man or the woman

☐ an article on women's liberation

☐ . . . .

☐ a leaflet for a commercial school

Where are the two people in the photo sitting?

☐ in a room in a private house

☐ in an office

☐ in a shop that sells office furniture

☐ . . . .

☐ in a conference room

What's your first reaction to the picture? What do you think the relationship between the two people is? Do you think it's a realistic picture?

Use your imagination   What office equipment or machines are there in the room? What other pieces of furniture are there? What kind of atmosphere has the room got? What sort of building is it in? Which other people are nearby? Where are they? What are they doing? What is the man in the picture doing? What is the woman doing? What is the man wearing? And the woman?

Talk to a partner   Talk to a partner and ask him/her

- if he/she has ever worked in an office
- for a description of a good boss
- for a description of a bad boss
- for a description of a good place to work
- which job or role in life has been the most important to him/her
- if he/she thinks the traditional roles of the two sexes are acceptable

Group opinion   Work in groups of 3 or 4.
Your boss has asked you to arrange several things. Decide in which order it would be best to do them.

. . . make sure of exact time of conference

. . . order taxi from office to airport

. . . book homeward flight

. . . order taxi from airport to conference centre

. . . make sure of exact place of conference

. . . book outward flight

. . . check the conference programme

. . . book room in hotel

Is there anything else you could arrange for your boss? What details must you give him/her? What other helpful information could you find out?

What about you?   How do you feel about the woman being the boss and the man being the secretary? What about the man staying at home and the woman going out to work? In which situations or activities do you think you would not be comfortable because of your sex?

Write about it   For some reason you aren't happy in the place where you work or where you study. Write a letter to a friend, who doesn't know your situation at all, and explain to him/her what is wrong.

Think about the picture

In your opinion, how does this woman look?

☐ calm ☐ thoughtful ☐ unhappy ☐ as if she's concentrating

☐ sad ☐ northern European ☐ happy ☐ . . . .

☐ serious ☐ southern European ☐ bored

Where is she and what is she doing? Why is she doing this?

Use your imagination

What is this building like inside? What objects can be seen there? Why is this woman all alone? What is she holding in her hands? What is the book she has in front of her? How often does she come here? What else does she do in this building? Why is this place important to her? How does she feel at the moment? How would you feel if you came in and saw her?

Talk to a partner

Talk to a partner and find out

- when he/she last went into a religious building, and for what reason
- if there is anything he/she particularly likes or dislikes about such buildings
- what his/her religious beliefs are now
- if his/her relationship to religion has changed much over the years

Group opinion

Work in groups of 3 or 4.
What do you think the work of religious groups should really be? How could they become more popular? What things do some people find hard to accept about religion today? Make a list of things a local group could do which would attract a lot of people to it.

What about you?

How much do you know about religious beliefs and traditions in your country and in other countries? Describe anything special that you know or have seen to the others in your class. Collect together all the information that you hear so that you can then make some comments on the similarities and differences that exist. Don't hesitate to ask questions if you think somebody else can give you an answer.

Write about it

Write a short description of a religious building that you've seen and liked. This building could be in your own country or in another country. Include some information about the outside of the building, the inside and also the atmosphere that existed in it.

Think about the picture   Where do you think this queue leads to?

☐ to an office   ☐ to a person   ☐ to a shop

☐ to a sports ground   ☐ to a large public building   ☐ . . . .

How do you think the people in this queue feel?

☐ bored   ☐ happy   ☐ afraid

☐ hopeful   ☐ angry   ☐ . . . .

Think of a situation where you might have the above feelings when standing in a queue. What do you think these people are queueing up for?

Use your imagination   What could some of these people be doing to pass the time? Is the queue moving very quickly? Which country is this in? Describe the street the people are standing in. How do the people first react when they join the end of the queue? What might their reactions be when they reach the front of the queue?

Group opinion   Work in groups of 3 or 4.
Answer these questions for the six other queues described below.
a) Who are the people who are queueing? What do they look like?
b) What is the general atmosphere of the queue like?
c) What will the people's reactions be, and what might the consequences be for them if they don't get what they've been waiting for?
d) Is there any danger of the queue getting out of control?

The queues:

● a queue to see the body of a popular politician who has been murdered
● a queue for food in a country where people are very hungry
● a queue to get into the first night at a theatre
● a queue for the bus (the only one today!)
● a queue for factory jobs in an area with very high unemployment
● a queue of people trying to leave a country for political reasons

Talk to a partner   You are both standing in a queue, next to each other, but have never met before. Decide what sort of queue it is, and then make a list of the things you might talk about – in the order in which they would be mentioned.

What about you?   What is your reaction when you have to wait somewhere for a long time? What can you do to make waiting more enjoyable? Can you remember ever having waited for a very long time? What was it for? What's the longest time you're willing to wait? What is the general attitude towards queueing in your country?

Write about it   You have been waiting for someone you'd arranged to meet in the foyer of a large international hotel. This person hasn't arrived. Write a message to leave at the reception desk. Tell the person how long you've been waiting, why you're leaving now and perhaps how he/she can contact you (if you want them to do that!).

Think about the picture   Who do you think this man is?

☐ a professional musician

☐ an amateur musician

☐ a student of music

☐ a music teacher

☐ a member of a local
orchestra or band

☐ a competitor in an international music
competition

☐ a pop musician

☐ . . . .

How many musical instruments do you know? Describe them. Which ones do you
specially like?

Use your imagination   What do this man's face and his gestures tell you? What is he looking at? Where is he
now? What sort of people are listening to the music being played? Describe the
audience in as much detail as you can. How often do these people play in public?
How does the man feel about being a member of this group of people? What has he
spent a lot of time doing in the past? Are all the people in the group of the same age
and sex?

Group opinion   The man in the picture could use all these words to talk about his musical activities.
Try and work out or find out what they mean.

music stand	the stage	tuba
conductor	the score	to improvise
to practise	notes	brass
to rehearse	the baton	to blow

Which of these words could also be used by a violinist to describe his/her activities
and instrument?

Talk to a partner   Talk to a partner and find out

- what sort of music he/she enjoys listening to
- for what reason and when he/she listens to music
- if he/she has ever learnt to play a musical instrument
- which instrument he/she would like to be able to play

What about you?   What are your feelings about the following kinds of music?

opera	jazz	rock and roll
disco	classical	country and western
folk	pop	

Write about it   Imagine you have been to a concert of any type of music (choose the type of music
from the list in the section above). Write a short report about the concert for your
local newspaper. Give some details about the music, the musicians and the people in
the audience.

Vocabulary suggestions

Unit	Some suggested vocabulary areas	Some vocabulary for the written task
1	holiday places; description of buildings e.g. materials, style, shape; description of atmosphere of a village or town; finding out and exploring	quiet, peaceful, quaint, deserted, relaxing, fresh air, panoramic view, hilly, romantic, primitive, old-fashioned, narrow, lazy, cool, steep
2	simple tools; simple way of life; description of complicated, highly-developed way of life; feelings about poverty; feelings towards less fortunate people	to miss something, to be better off, an adventure, satisfied, inventive, to get used to something, medicine, vaccinations, to settle down, to admire someone, expectations
3	writing letters; reactions to news; difficult letters; tactful expressions to put in a difficult letter	to apologize, honest, disappointed, to let someone down, to blame someone, unexpected, inconvenient, unplanned, to reply, to hurt someone's feelings
4	winter; the seasons; weather conditions; physical aches and pains that can be related to the weather	warm and sunny, cold, rainy, humid, windy, light clothes, warm clothes, raincoat, anorak, scarf, gloves, waterproof, boots, to wrap up well
5	phones; attitudes towards using the phone; instructions for using the phone; some expressions used on the phone	receiver, slot, coins, dial, dialling tone, directory enquiries, the operator, to be cut off, the wrong number, to get through, out of order, code, to insert
6	art galleries; different forms of art; reactions to art; museums; other tourist attractions in a large town	it isn't allowed, chew chewing gum, forbidden, to supervise, to touch, to run around, restrictions, meeting place, picnic facilities, work sheets
7	learning a foreign language; learning methods; schooldays; likes and dislikes of learning English; school subjects; activities that are part of learning	lesson, unit, chapter, test, to check the homework, to revise, to practise, to discuss, cassette, to be confused, to succeed, to fail
8	police; crime; reporting an event seen; description of people's appearance; description of clothing	to grab, to run away, shocked, to fall over, to brake, to skid, to hit, to injure, to look after someone, to call an ambulance, to swerve, to avoid
9	illness; looking after the sick; attitudes towards the sick; description of a room; description of a person's condition; some medical terms	to make sure, essential, self-discipline, to do you good, relax, stress, digestive system, wholefood, junk food, to avoid, to get exercise, physical health, mental health
10	old and young people; relationships between old and young; childhood; toys; description of a person's character; physical descriptions of people	to enjoy, to work together, to help each other, to pass the time, to babysit, to look after, to be close, alone
11	restaurants; descriptions of restaurants; food; people without food; people with too much food; eating habits; cooking procedures	to wash, to slice, to boil, to fry, to roast, to simmer, to mix, to brown, to grill, to stir, to cover, saucepan, frying pan, casserole, dish, to cut, to serve

Unit	Some suggested vocabulary areas	Some vocabulary for the written task
12	flats and houses; description of buildings; description of rooms; living conditions; features of home; living requirements; home-hunting	bathroom, fridge, towel, help yourself, the nearest . . ., emergency, neighbour, just round the corner, to search around, make yourself at home
13	solving problems; reactions to news; talking over problems; relationships to others; difficult conversations; problem areas; intimate problems	a difficult situation, confused, lonely, to be able to cope, support, isolated, to give some advice, helpless, inadequate, to turn to someone
14	airports; airport facilities; holidays past and future; planes; fears and nervousness	more seating accommodation, loudspeakers, staff, to organize, queue, practical, to improve, to do a survey, safety, security, high season, low season
15	cinema; types of film; films, TV and video; entertainment; description of places of entertainment; descriptions of films; reactions to films	audience, queue, ticket office, sold out, elegant, crowded, programme seller, usher, to chatter, group, row, aisle, stage, foyer, auditorium
16	developments; comparing the old and the new; progress; changes in people	standard of living, modern convenience, a necessity, indispensable, a waste of time, a time-saver, communication, to improve, to outweigh
17	travelling by train; travel in general; remembering and forgetting	to forget all about something, to be alarmed, essential, to remind someone, to cause trouble, to waste time
18	working conditions; routine work; jobs; job descriptions; contract conditions; employers and employees	experience, suitable, willing, to type, foreign languages, to like dealing with people, to work shifts
19	close friends; saying goodbye; childhood activities; older relatives	a close relationship, to be fond of someone, to love someone, to be an inspiration, to respect someone, proud
20	meeting people socially; description of groups of people in various social situations; national food and drink	spicy, fish, meat, vegetables, delicious, to serve a meal, mouth-watering smell, appetite, uninteresting, typical meal, delicate, flavour
21	sadness and comfort; emotions, reactions, feelings; crying; atmosphere in clinics and hospitals; description of buildings	to relax, to take my mind off the problems, contrast, to meditate, alone, to socialize, entertainment, to spoil oneself, a treat, to be tense, to be worried
22	hobbies; dangerous sports; sports and pastimes; taking risks; responsibility	foolhardy, irresponsible, unnecessary risks, exciting, accident, injured, paralysed, unable to work, ruined lives, challenge
23	contrasts in people in society; fashion; items of clothing; description of clothes; types of shops; shopping for clothes	loose clothes, sportswear, elegant, tight clothes, cotton, synthetic materials, silk, wool, colour combinations, formal clothes, smart clothes, casual clothes

Unit	Some suggested vocabulary areas	Some vocabulary for the written task
24	escapism; the unknown; childhood adventure; curiosity; description of doors; symbolism of doors	a scream, a strange sound, whispering voices, a sudden loud bang, to turn and run, slowly, carefully, afraid, expectantly, to laugh, to be shocked, to be horrified
25	male and female roles; personal characteristics; description of offices; boss/secretary and boss/employee relationship	dissatisfied, overworked, lazy, to be fed up, to want a change, to get on well with someone, boring, routine, uninspiring, to hand in one's notice, improvements
26	religions; religious buildings; the outsides and insides of religious buildings	made of stone, stained glass windows, spires, steeples, decorative, plain, simple, tall, impressive, ancient, carved figures, steps
27	queueing and waiting; description of people; passing the time	to hang around, to pass the time, to wander round, irritated, angry, disappointed, in a hurry, impatient, patient
28	music; musicians; concerts; types of music; likes and dislikes in music	musicians, stage, performance, conductor, audience, magnificent, disappointing, soloist, performer, technicians, applause, choice of programme

Further notes: Casablanca

The full story of Casablanca (1943) is too complicated to tell here. The two people in the picture are Rick, played by Humphrey Bogart, and Ilsa, played by Ingrid Bergman. The action takes place in Casablanca where there is a great business in travel documents for people wanting to leave Europe because of the Nazi occupation. Rick is a risk-taker and helps a lot of people to leave. The film turns into a romance when Ilsa arrives in Casablanca with her husband who is an important figure in the underground movement. Rick and Ilsa had been in love in Paris, and the picture shows them looking out of the window of a Parisian restaurant watching the first signs of Nazi occupation. They had planned to go away together, but at the last minute Ilsa didn't keep their appointment because she discovered that her husband, who she thought was dead, was alive. In Casablanca they realize that they still love each other and it is never actually clear until the end whether Ilsa is going to leave Casablanca with her husband or leave with Rick. In the end Ilsa is persuaded that her husband's work in the underground movement is more important than romance, and she leaves with him. The film was very successful at the time when it was made and has since become one of the classics, and one of Humphrey Bogart's best-known films.